Bennett's Point Resort, Oyster Bay, Campbell River

View from B.C. Government Ferry

It Pays to Play

BRITISH COLUMBIA IN POSTCARDS

1950s —1980s

Peter White

PRESENTATION HOUSE GALLERY / ARSENAL PULP PRESS

Vancouver

The book *It Pays to Play: British Columbia in Postcards, 1950s – 1980s* has been co-published by Presentation House Gallery and Arsenal Pulp Press in association with an exhibition at Presentation House Gallery from February 24 to March 31, 1996. The project is supported by the Canada Council's Exhibition Assistance Program.

EXHIBITION TOUR ITINERARY Dunlop Art Gallery, Regina Public Library, Regina, Saskatchewan, June 28 to September 15, 1996; Galerie Oboro, Montréal, Québec, February 22 to March 23, 1997; Kamloops Art Gallery, Kamloops, British Columbia, April 17 to June 1, 1997.

Presentation House Gallery is a non-profit cultural organization which receives annual support from the City of North Vancouver, the District of North Vancouver, the District of West Vancouver, the North Shore Arts Commission, the Greater Vancouver Regional District, the Province of British Columbia through the British Columbia Arts Council, and the Canada Council. Arsenal Pulp Press receives support from the Canada Council and the Province of British Columbia through the British Columbia Arts Council.

PRESENTATION HOUSE GALLERY
333 Chesterfield Avenue
North Vancouver, British Columbia
Canada, V7M 3G9

ARSENAL PULP PRESS
103 - 1014 Homer Street
Vancouver, British Columbia
Canada, V6B 2W9

CANADIAN CATALOGUING IN PUBLICATION DATA
White, Peter
    It pays to play

Based on an exhibition originated by Presentation House Gallery
    ISBN 1-55152-037-0

    1. Postcards—British Columbia—History.
2. British Columbia—Pictorial works. I.
Presentation House Gallery
II. Title.
NC1878.7.C3W54 1996   971.1í04í0222
C96-910482-0

EDITING/PUBLICATION COORDINATION:
Karen Love with assistance from Brian Lam
DESIGN AND PRODUCTION: Alexandra Hass
PRINTING: Kromar Printers, Winnipeg

PUBLISHER'S NOTE: While preparing this book Presentation House Gallery has made every effort to ensure the accuracy of all aspects of the publication, including illustration credits. Because of the nature of this material it has not always been possible to locate complete credits. Addenda, if available, will appear in subsequent editions.

Printed and bound in Canada. Distributed by Arsenal Pulp Press, Vancouver.

COVER:
Trail - Commerce, Industry and Recreation unlimited

CONTENTS

Pyramid Point

PREFACE

IT PAYS TO PLAY, THE TITLE OF THIS BOOK, IS A PITCH ON A COMMERCIAL postcard made for a company that sold billiard tables. The postcards that are the subject of the book are mostly scenic or view cards but that line somehow stuck, in part because they too are pitches. Made for tourists, the overriding attraction to which they refer is a process of modernization that transformed North American society in the years after the Second World War. In these cards, life is absorbed in an image of play that seems to be its own justification and reward. As it happens, these images also absorb the commercial values and many of the social instabilities, or pathologies, that belie the idea of life as play. Before the half-a-million-dollar Vancouver bungalow, before Douglas Coupland or the Internet, before land claims, Clayoquot and the myriad issues that make up the complex, highly negotiated terrain of contemporary life, this was an era that has proven to be as naïve as it once seemed hopeful.

For some this is a lost moment associated with youthful optimism and, perhaps, a more uncomplicated kind of life. For others it is no doubt a suffocating time they prefer would be forever vanquished, something that visiting these cards will no doubt reconfirm. As a baby boomer, my hope is that the book captures something of the mixture of affection and dismay with which I experience that era. My intention has not been to unburden yet more boomer self-absorption or angst but to offer some reflection upon the ideological inclinations of that time that may be of relevance as we consider those of our own era.

This book is the fruition of a project that began several years ago as a proposal for an exhibition at Presentation House Gallery. I am indebted to the gallery's director, Karen Love, for her complete support and faith in this idea. I am also appreciative of the significant commitment that has been made by Brian Lam and Arsenal Pulp Press. I had always thought there was an interesting book here, but never dared hope it would actually be realized. Many have shared their curiosity and provided assistance. In addition to the funding agencies, I would like to thank, in particular, Gisele Amantea, Bob Kite and Steve Knight of Lawson Mardon Packaging, Dr. Richard Moulton, David MacWilliam, Cyndy Chwelos, Michael Morrison, Robert Keziere, John O'Brian, Alex Hass, and, at the gallery, Linda Chinfen, Karen Derkach, Lianne Payne, Roman Pearce, Chris Rafuse, Susan Byman and Diane Evans. I would also add my thanks to those companies and individuals who have so generously granted permission to reproduce the postcards in the book.

Snow Scene, First Street, Revelstoke

INTRODUCTION

DURING RESEARCH FOR THIS BOOK, I WAS SURPRISED BY HOW MANY references I kept finding to the postcard. I was more surprised, however, by their tone. From high and low, left and right, it seems there are a lot of people out there who really don't like postcards. To the French philosopher Jacques Derrida, they're insidious. "And yet, there is nothing but post cards," writes Derrida. "It's terrifying."[1] According to the photographic historian and theorist John Tagg, unless photographs are understood to be "historically and institutionally produced," all you have are "bits of chemically discolored paper or, more to the point . . . , just a bunch of postcards."[2] I didn't necessarily expect uncritical affection. It's not for nothing that postcards are synonymous with the shallow and superficial. But do they really warrant this kind of disdain?

In a comparison of the souvenir and the collection in her influential book, *On Longing*, the American literary theorist Susan Stewart comes down on the side of the souvenir. Whereas the souvenir is a material residue of a particular emotional experience, objects in a collection gravitate to the impersonal framework of the series. As increments of more important wholes, any independent value they might have is all but nullified. It will probably come as no surprise that there are those who identify the postcard more with the collection than the souvenir.[3] And then there's Grace Metalious, author of *Peyton Place,* the celebrated fifties tell-all. "To a tourist these towns look as peaceful as a postcard. But if you go beneath that picture, it's like turning over a rock with your foot – all kind of strange things crawl out."[4]

Criticisms of the postcard may be many, varied and not necessarily without validity, yet how has something this outwardly banal earned its reputation as a cultural bottom feeder? My own sense is that it is the postcard's rather devious relationship to reality. Part of this has to do with the point Metalious makes. Despite the fact that the postcard appears to render an image of empirical reality, not only does it fail to describe reality, but it actually seems to cover up what is really going on. In this sense, the postcard isn't just devious, it's fraudulent. This criticism has been levelled at many forms of realist representation, notably the photograph, of which the postcard is a variant. But the postcard represents a perhaps more extreme case because of its unambiguously promotional nature. Its claim on reality is not so much documentation as authentication. Unless a postcard conveys a sense of "It was worth it" as well as "I was there" it will not have a very long shelf life.

But this is not the end of it. The idealizations and stereotypes of the postcard are representational conventions that are generally understood for what they are. The difficulty is that, like other forms of mass media, the constant circulation and repetition of the postcard naturalizes its images to a point where the reality it depicts can seem not only more compelling, but more real than actual experience. We are all familiar with the sentiment that a visit to a famous place doesn't live up to a pre-existing image or expectation we may have of it, or that a certain view or site would make a great postcard. It is here, as simulacrum, that the postcard really sticks in the craw. In effect, it succeeds all too well in its feel-good mission, flattering our desires despite our best defences or better judgment. To be blunt, it can make fools of us.

Aspects of this process have been analysed in a somewhat different context by the art historian Ann Bermingham in her work on the beloved nineteenth-century English painter John Constable. Referring to Constable's naturalistic rustic landscapes, Bermingham notes that these works present "an illusory account of the real landscape while alluding to the actual conditions existing in it."[5] Part of Bermingham's point is that this contradiction, this representational two-step or gap, is ideologically loaded. In the case of Constable's paintings, his choice of a pastoral subject and the "natural" way it is represented embody a specifically class view of landscape grounded in particular social and economic values.

Bermingham's observations are well taken. They point to the fact that while postcards may be banal, their fictionalized quotations of reality are not altogether innocent. In the case of postcards of British Columbia in the postwar period, a compelling image emerges of a decidedly middle-class society coming of age. Overriding value here is placed on aspirations for prosperity, growth, well being – in short, the good life – predicated on the wealth generated by industry, enterprise and an embarrassment of natural resources. Moreover, when such attitudes are invested in a medium that has such constant presence and is this widely distributed, it is apparent that a sense of identity, indeed, a particular view of life, is being actively produced, not simply reflected. Rather than a noun, the postcard might be thought of as a verb; instead of an image, as a social fact.[6]

A significant development during this time was the introduction of technologically sophisticated and relatively inexpensive means both to take and reproduce colour photographs. If the world was changing, so was the way it was seen. Prior to this, postcards were hand coloured or simply printed in black and white. Photographic colour brought an enhanced, vivid opticality and apparent naturalism to the postcard. Widely appealing, the new colour cards – known in the trade as "chromes" – not only interacted in significant ways with an emerging world of leisure and tourism, but they were absolutely in touch with the positive feelings and sense of possibility of the times. Not coincidentally, chromes are also referred to as "modern" cards.

This book, then, is an examination of how prevailing ideological biases, symbols and cherished myths during British Columbia's boom years following the Second World War were represented in postcards. It is about how knowledge, belief and value are constructed and how they are organized and operate socially through popular forms of representation. If, unlike most books that deal with postcards, this one does not have celebration or defence as a subtext, neither is it intended as a putdown. In her reflections on the postcard, the critic Naomi Schor has noted that readings of representation have swung in recent years to quite rigid, totalizing notions that understand all representation in terms of coercion. Schor argues that there are "lighter modes of social control," among which she counts the postcard.[7] The view is one I share, as is the implication that even if postcards, as Schor puts it, are "shot through" with ideology, that is not to say they cannot also be a source of pleasure. At the same time, this book is not intended as a social history, or at least the nostalgic kind that draws on the charm of postcards to illustrate life in a bygone era.[8] *It Pays to Play* may be read, however, as an index of dominant social attitudes from the climactic years of modernity, a period in which, in retrospect, an optimism buoyed by utopian ideals of progress and expansion seemed to be slipping away even as it had only begun to take hold. In this, with its bittersweet disjunctions between subjective experience and objective fact, the postcard was a form of modernist representation *par excellence*.

To draw out these attitudes, I have tried to make these otherwise familiar images "strange."[9] Beyond identifying the general pattern of historical references, common concerns and values that motivated different compositional strategies and motifs, this has involved placing cards in a variety of relationships and configurations, in some cases isolating them or making it possible to read them against themselves. While the general categories — landscape, leisure, urbanization and architecture, industrialization — may be straightforward, the contexts in which the cards appear are intended to play upon their contradictions and, I hope, tweak their apparently seamless surfaces. Indeed, whether we like or dislike them, whether they are a guilty pleasure or simply a pleasure, what makes these cards so interesting and, more to the point, revealing, is how they paper over contradictions they may recognize but cannot, of course, state. Interestingly, any number of subjects that might not have been anticipated — at least in terms of what postcards are generally thought to be about — also come forward. In addition to class, these include attitudes about nature, gender, the family and race. There are even glimmerings of alienation and disaffection, telltale signs of modernity's downside. I would like to think that as the author of one of the opening broadsides of the sexual revolution, Grace Metalious would be pleased. But then, it is not altogether coincidental that the era being scrutinized here overlaps with hers.

I also want to mention why this book is about British Columbia. One reason is purely practical. This material was first brought together as an exhibition at Presentation House

Gallery in North Vancouver.[10] With the show, I was anxious that viewers could respond to images that were familiar and therefore had some immediacy. Given the remarkable ubiquity of the postcard (*qua* Derrida), confining the exhibition to British Columbia also made sense. Yet it is clear that the approach taken here could readily be applied to a jurisdiction other than British Columbia. The experience that is described is a part of and in many ways relevant to a common North American culture. Beyond this, however, British Columbia has proven to be an ideal subject. The province's remarkable geographic diversity, its scale, beauty and forgiving climate made it a compelling destination during these years, as did Vancouver, its picturesque metropolis in the making. At the same time, the province's rich resource base fed the growth of many existing and new communities and businesses that were actively promoted as part of the new economic order. It is said that British Columbia is a collection of distinct regions existing in physical and perhaps psychological isolation from each other. Yet, tucked between the Rocky Mountains and the Pacific, the province also provides a clear focus as a natural and recognizable entity. I might add that I don't know whether more postcard images were made of British Columbia during these years than of other provinces or parts of the world. I do know, however, that I had an opportunity to look at a lot of postcards working on this project and can safely say that those of British Columbia cover virtually every representational trick in the scenic postcard repertoire. Whether this is a blessing or a curse is another question.

1   Quoted in Naomi Schor, "*Cartes Postales*: Representing Paris 1900," *Critical Inquiry* 18 (Winter 1992), 241.

2   Joanne Lukitsh, "Practicing Theories: An Interview with John Tagg," in Carol Squiers, ed., *The Critical Image: Essays on Contemporary Photography* (Seattle: Bay Press, 1990), 232.

3   See Schor's discussion of this question, "*Cartes Postales*," 200–03; Susan Stewart, *On Longing: Narratives of the Miniature, the Gigantic, the Souvenir, the Collection* (1984; Durham and London: Duke University Press, 1993).

4   Craig Nelson, *Bad TV: The Very Best of the Worst* (New York: Dell, 1995), 36.

5   Ann Bermingham, *Landscape and Ideology: The English Rustic Tradition, 1740–1860* (Berkeley and Los Angeles: University of California Press, 1986), 3.

6   The distinction between noun and verb in terms of the representation of landscape is made by W. J. T. Mitchell in his introduction to Mitchell, ed., *Landscape and Power* (Chicago and London: University of Chicago Press, 1994). The characterization of representations as social facts has been made by the British cultural theorist Stuart Hall.

7   Schor, "*Cartes Postales*," 192-93. My thoughts about this and a number of other aspects of the postcard are indebted to Schor's wide-ranging and insightful essay.

8   See, for example, Allan Anderson and Betty Tomlinson, *Greetings from Canada: An Album of Unique Canadian Postcards from the Edwardian Era 1900-1916* (Toronto: Macmillan of Canada, 1978). Although it involves a genre not considered in this book, a more analytical approach to the postcard is taken in Roger L. Welsch, *Tall-Tale Postcards: A Pictorial History* (Cranbury, New Jersey, and London: A.S. Barnes and Company, 1976).

9   John O'Brian has used the idea of making images "strange," that is, altering the usual context in which they are viewed. This approach was taken in the presentation of a wide variety of images for the exhibition *Capitalizing the Scenery: Landscape, Leisure and Tourism in British Columbia, 1880s-1950s*, Morris and Helen Belkin Art Gallery, University of British Columbia, September 29 – October 28, 1995. Please see O'Brian's comments in the exhibition brochure. The exhibition was organized by O'Brian and students from two of his art history classes at U.B.C.

10   The exhibition included more than two thousand postcards organized in similar but not identical categories as those in this book. The exhibition also included a selection of one hundred and sixty cards that were shown in enlarged form (five-by-eight feet) by means of continuous rear-screen slide projection.

Chinatown at Night, Vancouver

British Columbia, "Land of Opportunity"

It Pays to Play

THE PROMOTIONAL MESSAGES SUPPLIED ON THE BACKS OF POSTCARDS, written virtually as afterthoughts by itinerant commercial photographers, harried printshop salesmen or motel managers, are not without their charm. Nevertheless, they are rarely as interesting or revealing as the images on the other side. One of those exceptions is a card published by the British Columbia Government Travel Bureau that, chronologically, is almost certainly the earliest in this book. Its heading is:

BRITISH COLUMBIA, CANADA
"Land of Opportunity"

The message itself reads:
Old paddlewheelers still ply the Okanagan Lakes of British Columbia, but modern highways now also lead through this scenic wonderland.

The credit line indicates that the card:
. . . is furnished for convenience of men in the armed forces . . .

There is the further tag:
Write the Bureau for full information on British Columbia.

This card is a recruitment for a new era. With what might strike us now as an eerily familiar ring, British Columbia declares itself open for business. Ready access to even the remote interior is provided by up-to-date roads. Despite this, the old values still hold. Evoking a time of peace and quiet, paddlewheelers and the great beauty of the place are reassuring signs of continuity amid change. They aren't the only ones, however. Directed specifically to a male audience, the message also identifies the public domain of opportunity as masculine. After the widespread contributions they had made to the war effort, this is something that women, in particular, might reasonably have wondered about.

The image more than delivers on the enticements on the back of the card. Two "eligible" women are pictured lakeside, their views directed to the distant horizon. The double entendres this image sets up are something to behold, for it is clear that these women, not to mention the men to whom the cards are addressed, have their sights set on more than the scenery. The unpopulated, unspoiled landscape isn't the only virgin territory here and "opportunity" doesn't relate to prosperity alone. The car in the foreground of the image, practical yet somehow sexy and alluring, also seems to be working overtime, a sign of both social and physical movement.

Skipping ahead a few years, this time to the aptly named Miracle Beach, it is clear where all of this has led: the baby boom and the middle-class nuclear family, the basic social unit of the new era. Squarely facing the future, this family is an image of hope and possibility. It also enacts its own hierarchical structure. The hunky, protective father and his kids are central, demonstrably set off by the almost dowdy wife/mother in her straw hat and shift. Situated behind and to the side of her husband and children, a literal embodiment of the gender gap, she seems marginalized even within her own family. One wonders if she may be the prototype of the sexless fifties housewife who secretly manages her isolation and neuroses with pills and booze.

These two cards bring together a number of the postcard's main props during the postwar years as well as several of its basic themes. From a decidedly male point of view, the good life is specifically articulated in terms of the nuclear family, mobility and prosperity, which are intertwined with and somehow gauged by visible signs of consumption: cars and leisure set in endlessly beautiful landscapes beneath bright, permanently sunny blue skies. The optimistic and forward looking attitude of these images is of particular interest. Marked by atmospheric settings and obvious, dramatic staging, these cards don't seem quite real. The present seems to have been virtually displaced or deferred to a projection of an even brighter future. This current of equivocation and ambiguity is characteristic of the paradoxical experience of modernity. Built on dreams, its utopian impulses are caught on a perpetual and rather hopeless roller coaster of renewal and reinvention. In Marx's famous words, it is as if "all that is solid melts into air."[1] "To be modern," writes Marshall Berman, "is to find ourselves in an environment that promises us adventure, power, joy, growth, transformation of ourselves and the world – and at the same time that threatens to destroy everything we have, everything we know, everything we are."[2]

This is a process that is clearly evident in British Columbia. Following the war, the province underwent massive modernization. Led by W.A.C. Bennett, a hardware store owner who thought he had found paradise when he arrived in Kelowna before the war (from the Maritimes via Alberta), the province's activist Social Credit government staged a wide-ranging program of development.[3] First was the establishment of an enhanced transportation network – principally highways and a government ferry system – that linked regions of the province previously cut-off from each other while also opening up the North. This was followed by the construction of mega hydroelectric power and other large-scale infrastructure projects. In these upbeat economic circumstances, the province's resource industries, especially forestry and mining, underwent tremendous expansion. In

Miracle Beach Provincial Park, Vancouver Island

Rogers Pass

Rogers Pass

almost all areas of the province, urbanization and population also grew accordingly. No doubt it all seemed wonderful, even euphoric. Nevertheless, disquieting signs of disenchantment and diminished expectations were evident as early as the mid-1960s in the form of rising unemployment and creeping inflation. British Columbia historian Jean Barman quotes Robert Bonner, the province's Attorney General, at the time of his resignation in 1968: "We may have oversold it. Now there is a feeling there is no limit to what can be done . . . there is a failure to relate our expectations with our capacities."[4] Bonner's comments coincide with the student riots in Paris and the 1968 Democratic Party convention in Chicago, and are at or near the highwater mark of both the counterculture and the first wave of the women's movement. Greenpeace and a provincial New Democratic Party government were only a few years off.

It has been observed that modernization is not a sustained phenomenon but tends to move in irregular, often dislocating and disorienting cycles.[5] With a perhaps greater gap than other regions between its economic potential and level of development at the time the war ended, British Columbia had a lot of catching up to do. The rate and intensity of transformation of what Bennett liked to call "the last economic frontier" was remarkable. Within two decades the province went from a relatively isolated, regional backwater to previously unknown levels of economic dynamism and social comfort. Accompanied by political backlash and increasing social fragmentation, the pace of change slowed considerably beyond the 1960s. Nevertheless, the momentum of that initial surge carried over well into the 1980s. In terms of periodizing the modernization of British Columbia, if the beginning follows upon the conclusion of the war, the consecration of a post-industrial, global economy at Vancouver's Expo '86 probably marks a convenient end. The ebb and flow of this period is not apparent, however, in postcards of the era. Commercial postcards are obviously not equipped to deal with larger conflict or unrest that may exist in the landscape. While they rolled with the good times and were produced in large numbers through the 1960s, their production began to tail off in the following years. Instead, the more popular and better selling cards continued to be reissued in a postcard equivalent of golden oldies. Some remained in circulation for more than three decades. As a result, postcards produced their own kind of dislocation, retailing a cheery image through the 1970s and 1980s that not only was increasingly dated but more contradictory than ever.[6]

In terms of postcards, 1962 could be designated this period's centre of gravity. This is the year that the stretch of the Trans-Canada Highway through the Rogers Pass in Glacier National Park was completed. The opening of the Pass was recognized as a landmark event at the time. A major triumph of modern technology, not only did it finally link British Columbia by a major, direct road to the rest of the country, but it symbolically represented the end of the province's historic isolation and its emergence as a fully modern society. As a virtual pin-up for modernity, postcard immortality was bestowed on

Rogers Pass

Rogers Pass

the Pass almost immediately. Photographed from every conceivable angle and point of view, the postcards of Rogers Pass play out a kind of modernist parable. An establishing shot, as it were, features yet another family. Minus the mother this time but with the addition of a pet dog, the family is perched dramatically on a rocky outcrop overlooking the vast panorama of the mountain pass and the twisting ribbon of highway that stretches out before them. The general scenario will already be familiar, but the sense of expansiveness, of the freshness of the air, of uplift and earthly perfection are almost tangible. Panning to the road itself, there is a close-up of traffic as it swoops through the landscape. The feeling here is also tangible, but this time it is the thrill of speed and action. In modern life, nature seems to have been reborn, or at the least reshaped, as a human playground. Moreover, as a conduit for tourists and truckers alike, the best and perhaps most important thing here is how profitable it all is. Indeed, while play is usually thought of as a reward for work, in the postcard version of modernity, the terms tend to get telescoped, or simply reversed, with play becoming a visual sign for commerce and productivity. As industrial landscapes go, the Rogers Pass is subtle. But then, that's the point.

That this landscape might have a darker side has been conveniently suppressed, something that is evident in two winter scenes. To this day, travelling the Rogers Pass in winter can be perilous. Even when weather conditions are good, extreme caution is called for. You would never know it from these cards. In one, a young couple, flanking their poodle, appear to have stopped for a moment to admire the stunning mountain scenery. Like others of the genre, this card has inspirational overtones with definite intimations of the dawning of a new era. The other card is an image of a Volkswagen on its way up to the summit. The message of the card is clear enough: in the dead of winter, the same Volkswagen that had difficulty negotiating the driveway can make it through the mountains. This image says a great deal about the arrogance of attitudes towards nature but is loaded in another way. In the context of modernity, the inexpensive and popular Volkswagen represents not just the desire for, but the possibilty of individual mobility and freedom. It's not only that the Volkswagen can make it through, but that just about anyone can. This card may not eliminate the question of social hierarchy altogether, but it certainly blurs it in its projection of an all encompassing, undifferentiated middle class. Indeed, in this as in all of these images of Rogers Pass, the middle class seems to be the point of convergence not only for the possibilities of life, but also for a complete notion of what life should be.[7]

There is a paradox here, of course, because modern society thrives on distinction, if not conflict. People who drive Volkswagens and people who drive Cadillacs may both fall within the orbit of the middle class, but they occupy such different parts of it that the alienation, frustration or disappointment that are produced might be thought of as class rivalry by another name. This also raises questions about those who exist outside these terms of reference. One of the sexiest postcard images of Vancouver is a nighttime street scene of Chinatown aglow with coloured neon restaurant signs. It is an exotic image but, to be sure, no more so than other night scenes of the city. It is, however, virtually the only image of Chinese life in Vancouver in these cards. Just the opposite happens with references to the province's First Nations, who are represented primarily by an attribute, the totem pole. Both as subjects themselves and simply as part of the scenery, totem poles are incredibly ubiquitous in British Columbia postcards, so much so, however, that they begin to be read, like the people themselves, as invisible. One of the great ironies of a card of the "world's tallest totem pole" in Victoria's Beacon Hill Park is its remarkable lack of presence. It may be the world's tallest, but it also looks like the skinniest. While there is nothing as blatantly racist as the imagery found in postcards from earlier in the century, the very absence of native people, except through these totem poles, is striking in terms of the narrow and restrictive point of view of the "modern" postcard.[8]

The Beacon Hill totem pole raises another issue. One of the ways that the disruptive pressures of modernization express themselves is in an often powerful attachment to the past,[9] which is understood as a source of stability and security and tends to be experienced as nostalgia or longing for a golden age. This was evident in the descriptive text of the B.C. Government card set in the Okanagan. In a province with as little history as British Columbia, there are relatively few visual symbols that can be referred to. This may explain the number of postcards that feature totem poles. Lacking a history of its own, one is simply annexed. Moreover, given the traditions of romanticism that prevail, it is a history of nobility and grace that need not also refer to more difficult or sensitive social realities. In this postcard, the blending of the past with the present, which is represented by the car and its female driver, does not appear to be too smooth. In one sense, the image might be read simply as the kind of cheap visual pun that would be expected from a postcard: the rather ludicrous juxtaposition of the world's tallest totem pole and what looks like the world's smallest car. Nonetheless, there is an odd sort of equivalence. If the totem pole is attenuated, the car is not the full-size ideal of the time but, in fact, a kind of miniature or novelty vehicle that was being produced specifically with a secondary but growing women's market in mind.[10] In a way, it's a double putdown that reinforces the underlying ideology and real conception of power that is at large in these cards.

Another instance in which the signs have been scrambled with interesting results is a postcard of a new B.C. Government Trout Hatchery near Wardner. The dominant feature of the image is a large, abstract, rusted steel sculpture. A virtual commonplace in these years, sculptures of this type were usually commissioned, against the wishes of the public and politicians, for public buildings in urban centres as a demonstration that modernity not only had arrived, but that it had been embraced. The photographer who chose to take this shot might well be accused of as much confusion as the bureaucratic process that produced this lump of clichéd abstraction in the middle of nowhere. And yet there appears to be an undeniable logic at work. In the context of modernity, the introduction

World's Tallest Totem Pole in Beacon Hill Park, Victoria

of technology to increase and manage the supply of fish not only calls for commemoration, but it qualifies the site as a tourist destination. If the totem pole marks Beacon Hill with history, the trout hatchery's big steel confers the blessings of modernity on nature.

In many ways, the kind of imagery found in these cards goes back to the beginnings of the postcard in the nineteenth century.[11] This shouldn't be so surprising. Modernity may not be homogenous or have a completely smooth trajectory, but it does date at least to the industrial revolution. At the same time, the imagery of these modern cards is deeply entrenched in the formal strategies and emotional values of the romanticism of the last century. Like much television, advertising or the movies, scenic or topographic postcards have traditionally recycled in a refitted form the stock imagery of romanticism, be it the landscape itself, dramatic city skylines, views of picturesque towns or popular sites and beauty spots. The modern card differs from its forebears in at least one important aspect, however. In what is referred to as the postcard's golden age, from around the turn-of-the-century to somewhere beyond 1915, the postcard served an important documentary function, providing a primary popular source of visual knowledge of the world. As Schor notes, it was like "C N N , *People, Sports Illustrated*, and *National Geographic* rolled into one."[12] This role lessened with the onset of photographic reproduction in newspapers and magazines. Instead, the postcard was increasingly concentrated on and responsive to the growing world of tourism and its promotional requirements. The change after the Second World War was more one of degree than kind with major shifts taking place in the way life was lived and in photographic technologies themselves. As has been suggested, the "chrome" card was an ideal vehicle for the new way of life, its colour, brightness, sharpness, overall depth and life-likeness not only in keeping with the dynamism of the times but an expression of the technological magic that made it possible.

Life-likeness, however, is relative. During the Depression, for instance, a gritty black-and-white documentary style was thought to represent true photographic realism, as it has pretty much since. What it really captured, of course, was an ideological attitude. Similarly, the chrome represented a point of view consistent with dominant socio-economic values, its intense blues, lush greens and strategically placed concentrations of red directly tuned into the upbeat mood of the times. The significant role of colour during these years cannot be overestimated. Encompassing everything from kitchen appliances, vinyl furniture and other domestic design items to colour television and cars, the chrome was part of a largely commercial revolution associated with colour that culminated in the Pop era of the 1960s and 1970s. Into an everyday life that had been marked by the drabness of the Depression and the travails of the war years, colour introduced decorative variety, novelty, liveliness and, significantly, optimism. In terms of postcards, perhaps the greatest exponent of colour was the Irish photographer John Hinde. For Hinde, colour was a "life force."[13] He believed colour had the power to please people and developed a populist style that elevated colour to unmatched levels of vibrancy. Consistent with his equation

Trout Hatchery, Wardner

of colour with "positive feeling," classic Hinde cards push colour technologies to the limit. A distinctive three-dimensional, almost sci-fi effect is achieved through heightened, highly saturated colour that is all the more striking given the prosaic nature of most of the themes and subjects that are involved. Even the most casual viewer could not believe that what they were seeing was a mirror image, so far removed are these cards from the world they ostensibly depict.

Although there is nothing that quite matches Hinde's over-the-top passion in chromes of British Columbia – or anywhere else for that matter – similar principles apply. While much postcard photography is perfunctory at best, a surprising amount of it is of a remarkably high quality. Nevertheless, the work of the photo-etcher and the printer back in the shop was almost as important as that of the photographer. Not only did they produce the glossy look so essential to these cards, but they also were responsibile for the manufacture of stunningly blue skies in a land of rain and floral arrangements with a richness of colour that exceeds anything in nature, even British Columbia's. One rather blatant example, and perhaps all the more appealing for it, is a striking card of Emerald Lake in Yoho National Park. In a glorious affront to reality, the card is completely tinted green. Colour was not the only area where augmentation was practiced. Like postcards of an earlier era, but with the advantages of enhanced technical means, chromes take delight in reorganizing the world. Extraneous details – such as obtrusive telephone poles and other visual unpleasantries – are rigorously excised. As deemed necessary, even whole backgrounds are dropped out or in. With the needs of the composition always taking precedence, human figures and other key motifs, be they cars or just a convenient rose bush or flag, are positioned strategically for optimum effect. It goes without saying that photographs are taken from mostly dramatic though, it has to be said, never jarring angles. A far cry from how the world is actually experienced, these postcards are strongly crafted illusions designed to sell the wonder of their times and, therefore, themselves.

One of the defining colours of the colour revolution of the 1950s was pink. Highly popular, its mark was felt across a wide range of consumer products. One theory for the prominence of pink, pastels and any number of other delicate colours, was that they "reflected the image of soft femininity and exotica that characterised domesticity" during this decade.[14] No doubt they also countered, or at least mitigated, a modernist architectural aesthetic that was grounded in the principles of mass production and standardization and, at its extremes, conceived of the house as a machine to live in. With their repetitive, box-like designs, it's little wonder that the homes to which the suburban housewife was consigned needed some distinctive touches and softening of their otherwise hard edges. Not only is a strong sexual division between taste and design implied here, but it leads to the suggestion that pink, "linked with the idea of female childhood, . . . represented the emphasis on distinctive gendering that underpinned 1950s society, ensuring that women were women and men were men."[15] This division is further reinforced by the vision of

Emerald Lake – Mount Burgess

Florence Nightingale Private Hospital, Whalley

Blossom Time

Flamingo Drive-In Hotel, North Surrey

female sexuality for which pink was also a sign. The flip side of the image of the repressed housewife – a naughty notion of availability – is of course a thoroughly male fantasy. It should come as no surprise that what was true of other products was also true of the post-card. From dreamy fields of cherry blossoms to "Flamingo" motels and hotels, it seems no effort was spared to produce cards with a lot of pink.[16] To what extent these cards may have participated in the gendering process is difficult to ascertain. But it would be difficult to deny that they embodied these values, occasionally with results that are more than a little strange. Consider a postcard of the enterprising Florence Nightingale Private Hospital. An incipient example of rectilinear, modernist form, the hospital is trimmed in pink and set off by a shiny, high-finned pink Cadillac, a classic icon – and cliché – of the late 1950s. The message on the back of the card reads: "Deluxe accommodation for aged, chronic and convalescent patients. A Hospital with a friendly, homelike atmosphere." Talk about mixed messages. Maybe the postcard skeptics are right.

1   Marx's phrase is incorporated in the title of Marshall Berman's critical study, *All That is Solid Melts into Air: The Experience of Modernity* (1982; Penguin Books, 1988).

2   Ibid., 15.

3   My primary source for the history of British Columbia is Jean Barman's excellent *The West Beyond the West: A History of British Columbia*, ed. rev. (Toronto: University of Toronto Press, 1996). See especially the chapter "The Good Life," 270-96.

4   Ibid., 295.

5   Kristen Ross, *Fast Cars, Clean Bodies: Decolonization and the Reordering of French Culture* (Cambridge, Massachusetts, and London: The MIT Press, 1995), 4.

6   The period under consideration in the book also marks a distinct phase in the history of postcards. For the most part, the classic three and a half by five and a half-inch chrome has been superceded by glossier, larger format cards, many of which feature decorative framing designs and bold type on the image side. The new generation of cards seem as much greeting card as traditional scenic postcard. This is further reinforced by the optical sharpness of contemporary postcards that are produced digitally. At the same time, the number of producers has shrunk as postcards, like books, are increasingly being sent offshore for printing. With fewer local producers and a more global orientation to tourism generally, there are also far fewer images being produced as postcards.

7   Ross, *Fast Cars*, 10.

8   For examinations of the politics of representation in French colonial postcards, see Malek Alloula, *The Colonial Harem*, trans. Myrna Godzich and Wlad Godzich (Minneapolis: University of Minnesota Press, 1986) and David Prochaska, "Fantasia of the Photothèque: French Postcard Views of Colonial Senegal," *African Art* 24 (1991), 40-47, 98-99.

9   Ross, *Fast Cars*, 4.

10 Although she does not discuss the size of cars, Penny Sparke refers to the design and marketing of cars for women at this time. See Sparke, *As Long as it's Pink: The Sexual Politics of Taste* (London: Pandora, 1995), 198-99.

11 For a general history of the postcard, see Frank Staff, *The Picture Postcard and Its Origins* (New York: Praeger, 1967).

12 Schor, *"Cartes Postales,"* 193.

13 *Hinde*sight: *John Hinde Photographs and Postcards by John Hinde Ltd.* (Dublin: The Irish Museum of Modern Art, 1993).

14 Sparke, *As Long as it's Pink*, 195.

15 Ibid., 196.

16 No name was more popular for motels and tourist hotels during this period than "Flamingo." Five different Flamingos were included in the exhibition *It Pays to Play*. The association of Flamingos and good times probably owes a good deal to the fame of the Flamingo Hotel in Las Vegas. Built after the war, it was the first major hotel on what has become Las Vegas' famous "Strip."

Osoyoos Lake Overlook

LANDSCAPE

To experience modernity, the nineteenth-century poet Charles Baudelaire wandered the streets of Paris. In the second half of the twentieth century, we headed for the hills. The poet's immersion in the city and our escape from it were accompanied by a sense of breathlessness, even dizziness. However, if the source of Baudelaire's was the crowds, the upheaval and stirring public life of the changing city, ours was the sheer thrill of speed and the sensation of personal freedom with which we moved through the landscape in our much beloved cars. In effect, nature was understood in terms of the possibilities and demands of modernity. But then, this is a relationship with a history.

At a time when there is a strong consciousness of the world's environmental fragility, it may be difficult to imagine a time when the natural landscape wasn't a repository of our hopes, beliefs and deeply held values. Yet, it was only with the emergence of modernity that landscape began to occupy this role in the West. Associated with the eighteenth-century transition in Europe from what had been essentially a rural, feudal economy and social structure to a largely industrial, capitalist, democratic and increasingly urban way of life, modernity wrought complex changes. Among them were new, often intense pressures placed on the land to provide for the new economy, the increasing stratification of society on the basis of class, and the development of conceptions of individualism and liberty that were themselves tied to new freedoms, including the right to own property.

Discussing the emergence of aesthetics as a distinct branch of philosophy and thought at this time, Carole Fabricant has suggested that the aesthetic attitude towards nature is directly linked to these changes.[1] Divested of its traditional role in a fixed social order, landscape is filled with new meanings that tend to reinforce the self through an emphasis on the validity of individual perception. According to Fabricant, the aesthetic attitude espoused liberty not just politically but psychologically. The unfettered eye's freedom to roam combined a "grandeur and majesty normally linked to a traditional aristocracy with the liberty and mobility more congenial to the nouveaux-riches – to an expanding, prosperous capitalist class in the process of moving up into the world of the aesthetically cultivated, landed gentleman."[2] Implying human sovereignty over nature, this continuum of land, aesthetic sentiment and capitalism expressed a kind of middle-class espousal of energy, industry, movement, improvement and variety. It also established the principle that the greater the economic use and impact on the land, the greater the aesthetic fascination. As de Tocqueville observed in America, it was the consciousness of the destruction of nature that made it all the more desirable.[3]

In eighteenth-century England, these attitudes saw an often literal transformation of the landscape, epitomized on the one hand by the enclosure of lands for economic purposes and, on the other, by the development of landscape gardens, often on a vast scale, for seemingly aesthetic reasons. As Ann Bermingham has noted, "As the real landscape began to look increasingly artificial, like a garden, the garden began to look increasingly natural, like the preenclosed landscape."[4] With its preference for movement over stability and the idea that nature could be developed or shaped at will, this view of landscape is a fabrication that reflects the perceptions of this new class about society. Deeply ideological in its assumptions of possession and domination, it is a construction whose idealized imagery has had such resonance within the iconogery of romanticism that it has passed into common usage as if it were, indeed, natural. Ironically codified and standardized through the languages of the picturesque, beautiful and sublime and repeated endlessly in a variety of visual and literary forms, including the postcard, this conception of the natural landscape as a kind of personal property or, as one writer has put it, "a well-loved pet,"[5] has been a form of cultural memory or capital that is drawn upon and put into play whenever these images are employed. At the same time, as modernity has moved through its cycles, this vision of landscape has provided a sense of historical continuity and connection, something that is further reinforced by the powerful tugs of nostalgia that it can also trigger.

In the mid-1980s, the British Columbia government's advertising agency whipped up a particularly slick and aggressive campaign that touted the wonders of "Super, Natural B.C." The choice of words is revealing. Not only did it underline that a province with scenery as spectacular and abundant as British Columbia's is a romantic dream come true, but the transparency of its hype also carried a hint of doubt or hesitation. By this time, it was difficult to sell even British Columbia this way. This shift may put in perspective both the particular innocence and appeal to fantasy – personal and otherwise – with which the landscape was represented by the heightened look and intensified colours of the chrome postcard. Predictably, stunning views of mountains, rivers, lakes, forests, sea coasts, rolling hills, valleys, highland meadows and so on appear in these cards with a constancy that their great natural beauty would seem to demand. These motifs are pictured as individual sites, sometimes in conjunction or dramatic juxtaposition with each other, sometimes with neat touches like unbelievably symmetrical mirror images. The predominant colours are bright blues and greens but there are also a variety of lovely earth tones, all evenly bathed in the radiance of a warm, resplendent light. In these images, nature reads like a private or special garden, a refuge to which we have been given individual access and where we can enjoy the privilege of seeing without being seen.

Consistent with romanticism's traditional emphasis on the self, people are commonly pictured in postcards of the landscape. In one way these figures are putative viewers, their eyes guiding ours through the contours of the landscape while acting out our own identification or feeling of unity with nature. This is especially true of those images where figures are placed in the foreground looking out over the landscape and, often in the case of families or couples, to the future. Many cards feature children or young women who serve as handy metaphors for nature as a state of natural grace, purity or innocence. Also common are images of fully, sometimes highly sexualized women. The voyeuristic point of view of the postcard is perhaps never clearer than in these images, as is the gendering of the landscape. Decorum in the 1950s may not have allowed the commercial tourist postcard to go as far as the straight pin-up, but there is no doubt that it was the model upon which the coy suggestiveness of many of these cards played. Memorable among a litany of cuties is a knock-off of the blonde bombshell, another 1950s classic. Seen in half profile beside a curving canal that amplifies the remarkable fullness and roundness of her figure, she is wearing a pair of tight blue jeans and an even tighter red sweater. The use of strong shots of red in the foreground is a standard formal device in these cards. Complementary to the predominant greens of the background, they help to establish the depth of the image. In this case, however, red has something more than compositional significance. Indeed, an image like this brings together a number of the strands in a conception of nature that emphasizes manipulation and mastery. In the eighteenth-century English garden, Fabricant discerns a pattern of "freedom and constraint, abandonment and discipline. . . . Both women and landscape were continually being judged for their ability to titillate the imagination and satisfy the senses while at the same time remaining within carefully prescribed moral, aesthetic, and territorial limits."[6] Moreover, "Men of taste, leisure, and money, educated in how to see the world correctly, were understood to possess special privileges in relation to nature similar in many ways to a husband's conjugal rights."[7] These postcards may be from the twentieth century, but the underlying principles are largely the same. Equated with the feminine, nature in the modern world tends strongly to the sensuous, supple, compliant, submissive.

Proprietorial in our attitudes, when it comes to the car we have simply overrun and otherwise occupied the natural world. With the construction and improvement of roads and the onset of prosperity after the Second World War, the exploration of the landscape by car, already popular, became the *de rigeur* form of tourism in North America. As anyone who has crawled bumper-to-bumper, hour after hour, through the Rocky Mountains on a holiday weekend knows only too well, the call of the open road isn't always what it's cracked up to be. Nonetheless, in the carefree world of the postcard, where there is little traffic, the kids don't get carsick and desire is free to run rampant, this is not an issue. Once referred to by the architect Frank Lloyd Wright as "the horizontal line of freedom," the highway is a democratic trope that somehow seems to make physical and social mobility co-extensive.[8] Winding its way endlessly through, over and around the landscape that it transforms, it enjoys a similar prominence in the postcard. In many cards a sinuous stretch of road replaces the river or valley that artists had traditionally used to give movement, depth and feeling to their landscapes. More than a formal device, however, the road has been so integrated into the landscape that it has simply become a part of the scenery. Moreover, in some cards the road itself becomes the focus, the presence of blacktop not only crowding out nature but also conveying a palpable sensation of "panoramic perception." Described as occurring when "the viewer no longer belongs to the same space as the perceived object," panoramic perception refers to a suspension of time and contraction of distance, an "evanescent reality" in which "the perception of a detached world fleeting by a relatively passive viewer" is the norm.[9] No more engaged in nature, but enacting something other than the touristic gaze with motion added, the motorist passing through the landscape is a collector of fragmented views and disparate sights, badges of the elusive experience of modernity. Happily ensconced in the car and in control, the motorist is liberated yet insulated, cut off from the very disruption the automobile has created around it. The car in the landscape may figure as a contemplative space, but as these things go, it is definitely an ambiguous one.

1   Carole Fabricant, "The Aesthetics and Politics of Landscape in the Eighteenth Century," in Ralph Cohen, ed., *Studies in Eighteenth-Century British Art and Aesthetics* (Berkeley and Los Angeles: University of California Press, 1985), 49-81.

2   Ibid., 55-56.

3   Quoted in Barbara Novak, *Nature and Culture: American Landscape and Painting 1825-1875* (New York: Oxford University Press, 1981), 160.

4   Bermingham, *Landscape and Ideology,* 13-14.

5   Alexander Wilson, *The Culture of Nature: North American Landscape from Disney to the Exxon Valdez* (Toronto: Between the Lines, 1991), 33.

6   Carole Fabricant, "Binding and Dressing Nature's Loose Tresses: The Ideology of Augustan Landscape Design," *Studies in Eighteenth-Century Culture* 8 (1979), 109.

7   Ibid.

8   Wilson, *The Culture of Nature*, 32.

9   Ross, *Fast Cars*, 38-39.

Takakkaw Falls, Yoho National Park

The Lions, Vancouver

Moberly Lake

The Western Canadian Coast

Vasseaux Lake and McIntyre Bluff near Penticton

Mount Robson

Fraser River Canyon

Nicola Rangeland

Red Rock, Sinclair Canyon, Radium Hot Springs

Banff to Radium Highway

Crowsnest Pass Highway

#3 Highway between Creston and Nelson

Entrance to Stanley Park (causeway), Vancouver

Long Beach

Landslide on Hope-Princeton Highway

White Rock

M.V. Anscomb, Kootenay Bay

Oliver Canal

Vasseaux Lake

Pool, Kamloops Municipal Park

Spring Blossoms near Penticton

Thompson Canyon

Bridge to West Quesnel

Beacon Hill Park, Victoria

Hot Baths, Fairmont Hot Springs Resort

Night Scene, Vancouver

LEISURE

IT WAS A FAMILIAR MODERNIST MYTH. TECHNOLOGY WOULD GENERATE wealth while ridding people of the worst and most time-consuming aspects of work and labour. The result would be a surplus of free time and the affluence with which to enjoy it. From the perspective of an era that suffers from systemic underemployment and the global, twenty-four-hour work day, the extent to which this "dividend" was overly optimistic, at the least naïve, is only too apparent. So too perhaps is the complementary belief that in an industrially developed society, rest and leisure are basic human rights.[1] This was not, of course, evident in the immediate postwar decades. Quite the contrary. The opportunity to travel, to dine out, to self indulgently do nothing because it was good for one's soul - activities previously confined for the most part to the privileged - were widely indulged benefits of this period of assumed social democratization. The only problem seemed to be how people were going to cope with all of this leisure time.

Much of the discourse on tourism revolves around questions of consumption and authenticity. It is argued, for instance, that the motels, restaurants and other services that developed to meet the needs of a rapidly expanding tourist market replaced traditional social relations with commercial ones.[2] In this sense, the term hospitality industry is simply an oxymoron. As well, the translation of nature into something like a "leisure space," with a self-realizing experience of beauty as its product, has already been more than hinted at. Because it represents an attempt to discover an authenticity that has been lost in the modern age, there is also the suggestion that tourism is inevitably disappointing or unfulfilling.[3] What is lost cannot be recovered, especially when the need to do so is a response to what is being experienced as a lack of coherence or connection with something that feels whole. The result is only staged authenticity, figural rather than literal reality.[4]

These issues are unquestionably vital to a discussion of leisure. They also describe the condition of the commercial postcard and its representational conventions. However, this analysis cannot account for a temporal specificity that would seem to be crucial. The world of leisure that the chrome depicts was energized by a particular sense of discovery. Unquestionably innocent, it was nonetheless a powerful response to a new-found sense of possibility after an extended period of economic and psychological austerity. As well, this is a period that precedes widespread international travel, mass-marketed tourism and the homogeneity of fast food outlets, chain motels, superhighways, theme parks, heritage sites, and so on. An overwhelming percentage of pleasure travel in North America was being taken by car, most of it by individual families.[5] Motels were Mom and Pop operations and cafe lattes weren't being served at roadside rest stops.

It's not that the ideology underpinning the organization of leisure in this period should be ignored – the constrictions of the nuclear family, the monolithic social perspective, the very misleading promises to which these activities were a response. Nevertheless, it seems equally important to be mindful of the personal and cultural satisfactions these experiences provided as well as the burden of contempt that usually accompanies consideration of matters involving popular culture. One way of dealing with this challenge is to meet it head on. If leisure was understood as freedom from work, then it might be characterized as escape, or at least good escapist fantasy. The creativity this entailed is really rather remarkable. Take kitsch or, in this instance, its cousin the restaurant. The proliferation of thematic settings for dining – be they futuristic, South Pacific or rustic – may not have resulted in much of an improvement on the standard meat and potatoes diet, but surely it did wonders for the way it was consumed. Or consider a postcard of Eaton's Marine Room. It may seem a stupefying contradiction to combine in a single image a turkey buffet and a sophisticated model who looks like she has stepped out of the pages of *Vogue*, but copious amounts of food and daytime elegance speak to a formative sense of well being and pleasure. Or how about the roast that is the centrepiece of a promotional card for the dining room of Vancouver's Biltmore Hotel? However fetishistic it may be, it's well to remember that the apotheosis of the prime rib in these days also embodied significant social cravings.

No object or experience, however, catalyzed the impulse for fantasy like the car. As the primary force of modernization in this century, the car had an impact on social life which is inestimable. In its proliferation after the war, the car served a wide variety of symbolic functions. It connoted freedom, independence, affluence, productivity, technology, speed, glamour, good times, sex, to name only some of its most obvious meanings. Many of these happen to come together in a nighttime image of a single front fender heading in on a diagonal to a Granville Street lit up with neon as far as the eye can see. The glare of oncoming headlights, the sensation of motion, the softened outlines that result from illumination all conspire to produce an image of mystery and possibility, perhaps of something vaguely illicit. With the exception of landscape, no motif dominates these postcards like the car. But what is interesting is how it appears. As the subject of almost obsessional imaginative fascination, the car is consistently used to add its own special lustre to a wide variety of public spaces and subjects. One of the latter is the motel. Suggestively posed, the various Cadillacs, lesser American classics, muscle cars and stylish imports speak in an undisguised language to any number of tastes and expectations. The convention of the individually posed car has an obvious affinity with advertising, but has other interpretive possibilities. As the critic Kristen Ross notes, removed from the often negative, more realistic context of traffic, the isolated image of the car is a device that refers to the self, one that carries the symbolic weight necessary to make the individual feel special. More interesting, perhaps, is the suggestion that the car is a kind of liminal space, neither public nor private. A ritualized setting, it is a shifting mobile site for some of the most intense experiences and associations modernity has to offer.[6]

If escape carries with it an element of danger, this is a bet that is often hedged by the motel, a building type that exists because of the car. What is particularly striking about the motel, especially from the early years of this period, is its similarity to the very homes that have been left behind. With their simple, repetitive geometric designs and individual garages, some of these motels introduce a consciousness of the suburbs that further complicates the question of public and private space. While attractions like swimming pools – even those enclosed by chainlink fence – provide an experience that was not associated with the home, most of these motels testify to a kind of invasive domestication of nature. Here the question of consumption and authenticity are felt in all their reflexive force. Although their impact is similarly reflected in the representation of outdoor recreation, another growing leisure activity deeply affected by the car, their meaning is perhaps most fully explored by an image of a provincial government campground at Lake Okanagan. Tents, cars, campers, trailers aligned in a neat, tight arc – this is one of those conflicted images that are the special preserve of the modern postcard.

1   United Nations declaration on tourism, 1980. Cited by Wilson, *The Culture of Nature*, 19.

2   John Frow, " Tourism and the Semiotics of Nostalgia," *October* 57 (Summer 91), 150.

3   Although he sees it more positively, an influential proponent of the view that tourism is a search for a lost authenticity is Dean MacCannell. See MacCannell, *The Tourist: A New Theory of the Leisure Class* (London: Macmillan, 1976). MacCannell has been criticized for disregarding the socioeconomic dimension of tourism. See Frow, ibid., 129.

4   Frow, ibid., 125.

5   John A. Jakle, *The Tourist: Travel in Twentieth-Century North America* (Lincoln and London: University of Nebraska Press, 1985), 186-87. Although Jakle uses American statistics here, his book has a North American perspective and draws extensively on Canadian examples.

6   For a rich discussion of this subject in the context of modernization in France after the war, see Ross, *Fast Cars*, 15-70.

South Shore Motel, Okanagan Falls

View of Saanich Arm from the Malahat Chalet, Vancouver Island

Vancouver Auto Villas

Crest Motel, Victoria

Peacock Auto Court, Vancouver

2400 Motel, Vancouver

Buena Motel, Burnaby

Pacific Motel, Vancouver

Lougheed Hotel, Greater Vancouver

Sage Brush Motel, Kamloops

Grasslands Hotel, Merritt

Astor Hotel, Burnaby

Inter-City Motel, South Burnaby

Majestic (Motor) Lodge, Penticton

Mary's Motel, Golden

Ho Hum Motel, Princeton

Evergreen Motel, Princeton

The Diners' Rendezvous, Nanaimo

Polynesian Room, Waldorf Hotel, Vancouver

Tahitian Room Lounge, Waldorf Hotel, Vancouver

Menehune Banquet Room, Waldorf Hotel, Vancouver

Beverage Room, Maple Leaf Motor Hotel, Williams Lake

Stop & Go Inn, Cranbrook

Eaton's Marine Room, Vancouver

Biltmore Motor Hotel, Vancouver

A thrilling challenge

The Harrison Hotel

Skaha Lake

Copper Island, Shuswap Lake

Okanagan Lake, Kelowna

B.C. Forestry Camp, Okanagan Lake

Tyee Fishing, Vancouver Island

Branding Time in the Cariboo

Humpty Dumpty, Wooded Wonderland, Beaver Lake Park, Victoria

Osoyoos Cherry Carnival Parade

Kitsilano Showboat, Vancouver

Balfour Golf, Kootenay Lake

George's Glass Castle, Duncan

Empress Hotel, Victoria

The Bottle House, Boswell

B.C. Electric Building, Vancouver

URBANISM

ENTERING THE 1950S, TWO BUILDINGS DOMINATED THE VANCOUVER skyline – the Hotel Vancouver and the Marine Building. Actually, dominate is an exaggeration. For all their size, the chateau style of the former and stolid, early modern design of the latter gave them a somewhat dated appearance. As much as they stood out from the more modest buildings that surrounded them, they also blended in. All this changed, however, with the construction of the B.C. Electric Building, a sleek, glass tower that opened in 1957 at the corner of Burrard and Nelson. Not only was it Vancouver's first truly modern skyscraper, but the building's connection with the province's enormous, virtually untapped reserves of natural power made it a fitting, not to mention dramatic symbol of the era's commitment to progress. Along with a number of other landmark projects from this time – among them the multi-lane Granville Street Bridge, the new Public Library, the Queen Elizabeth Theatre – the B.C. Electric Building was an upbeat, public declaration that Vancouver was taking its place in a contemporary world of which it had never, in its isolation, totally felt itself a part. Like the others, it was and continued to be a highly popular postcard subject.[1]

Historically, urbanization has been one of the primary expressions of modernity. In the case of Vancouver, it followed a familiar North American pattern: as its skyline rose vertically, it spread horizontally, encompassing a vast region of suburban centres and malls connected by a growing network of roads and bridges. Yet the development of Greater Vancouver was only one aspect of urbanism in postwar British Columbia. Both the relative lack of agricultural lands and the need to situate people in proximity to outlying resources resulted in the growth of existing communities and the development of new ones beyond the Lower Mainland.[2] Well documented in postcards, not only is the representation of these communities significant in relation to the preoccupation with development and improvement at this time, but it is also revealing in terms of the dominance in this scenario of the metropolitan centre. As the lesser term in this equation, these regional centres carry a stigma that no amount of empirical evidence could hope to overcome.[3] Not that they didn't try. The expansion of the economy meant opportunity, and these communities were eager for their own piece of the action. Inevitably, the messages on the reverse of these cards tout the distinctive merits and attractions of the particular community. Produced with the new tourist market in mind but not confined to it, these cards proudly promote a quality of life. The message on a Port Alberni card is representative:

Looking up ARGYLE ST. with MT. ARROWSMITH in background – PORT ALBERNI is an important industrial center on VANCOUVER ISLAND with large pulp, plywood and shingle mills as well as extensive commercial fishing. In addition, the ALBERNI district offers the finest holiday activities and accommodation.

Although these places are represented by other views, the image that defines them is mainstreet. The mainstreet postcard is intended to convey a positive feeling through the manipulation of a number of stock features. There is, of course, the consistently warm and even light. The street itself forms a dynamic line between the stores that are lined up on either side of it while lively commercial signage provides a colourful effect and, through repetition, articulates movement or flow along the length of the street. Inevitably, however, these images come together around the car, both as a focal point in the street itself and as conspicuous and appealing elements stationed beside it. Although some of these images do manage to generate a feel for the bustle or industriousness consistent with the optimistic attitude they are intended to project, many feel surprisingly empty, sometimes to a point of strangeness. It's not exactly "The Twilight Zone," but there is a notable absence of people in these images. Focusing on commerce and cars, the predominant signs of prosperity, the historic context of mainstreet as a centre of exchange and community life is referred to, but then barely activated. Although the postcard wouldn't be expected to represent domestic life, this reductive view of the public domain does little other than reinforce the quaint, boosterish, one-dimensional image of smalltown life. Not only do these communities become virtually indistinguishable, but as modern places they operate as pale, virtuous reflections of a centre that is more glamorous, more creative and, most importantly, better off.

If the small town occupies a median position on modernity's axis of development, the communities of the North are located at its far end. In some ways, with their often unpaved streets, dusty cars and generally unfinished look, these towns have a rough-edged frontier spirit that has an undeniable romantic appeal. Yet their limitations are only too evident. Their streets seem even emptier and, as the incredible dreariness of a card of Cache Creek suggests, sometimes it's simply not possible to pull off the illusion of the good life. As for a remarkable bird's-eye view of the "instant" town of Kitimat, if its graphic clearcut is enough to make a contemporary viewer cringe, its newly planted tract houses are evidence of what an incredibly blunt social instrument economic opportunity can be. Serving many interests except their own, planned resource communities like Kitimat, not surprisingly, failed to live up to expectations.[4]

Compared to the frontier rawness of the North, Vancouver reads as a garden. While much of its architecture, its many green public spaces – especially Stanley Park – and mild, damp climate had always articulated its genteel English lineage, the city's gorgeous setting, its magnificent public beaches and overall physical lushness gave it an added new world drama. Yet it was only with the onset of the developments inaugurated in the 1950s that Vancouver seemed to be reaching its potential as a dynamic modern city with a future. The excitement generated by these projects was palpable. A card of the Granville Street Bridge that emphasizes its sweeping rampways and direct run-up to the downtown boasts that the eight-lane bridge is the widest on the continent "outside of New York." Vancouver undoubtedly absorbed its share of modernist disasters. The magnificently located, architecturally innovative, but functionally alienating campus of Simon Fraser University on Burnaby Mountain is an obvious example. Another is Granville Street itself, whose glorious run of neon was ultimately undermined by all the traffic that poured over the bridge. Nevertheless, the city probably could have done worse. After a freeway that would have cut through the heart of Chinatown was fought off in the 1960s, the city pretty much withdrew from the process of reorganizing itself spatially to accomodate the automobile, thus avoiding often devastating social side-effects that were experienced elsewhere. Moreover, Vancouver benefited from the paradox that however ugly, problematic or simply mundane much modern architecture can be, when it is all put together it can somehow be "one of the most exaltedly beautiful things man has ever made."[5] This is something clearly understood by the photographer of an overhead view of the city's West End, where much of the city's historic architecture was displaced by a sea of highrise apartments. With the North Shore, Burrard Inlet and the rising skyline of the transformed downtown in the background, the card makes a more than compelling case for the way of life this updated version of the city evokes.

A perhaps prototypical Vancouver postcard of this era is an image of the glittering geodesic dome of the Bloedel Conservatory, hovering like a flying saucer above the gardens of Queen Elizabeth Park. Notwithstanding this eccentric juxtaposition, the image testifies to a more or less fair trade-off, however contradictory, of the old, the new and the future in Vancouver. A more naïve example of this dalliance with the future is a cylindrical provincial government office building in Duncan. Looking as if it has been dropped in from the set of a sci-fi film, not only is the building isolated in its own plaza, but its regional location testifies to the remarkable missteps that could be taken in the application of alien – read universal – architectural styles to particular local contexts. Yet better this novelty, perhaps, than the functional boxes that are this period's primary architectural legacy. At the level of everyday life, it would be interesting to know whether the many additions of decorative colour to the white surfaces that this style of architecture demanded are signs of subversion or, simply, expressions of boredom.

1   Cards of these and other subjects related to the development of the city, such as the Second Narrows Bridge, were reprinted continuously well into the 1980s.

2   Barman, *The West Beyond the West*, 289.

3   Rob Shields, *Places on the Margin: Alternate Geographies of Modernity* (London and New York: Routledge, 1991), 3.

4   Issues facing these towns included the high cost of living, health problems related to industrial waste and social malaise resulting from isolation and dependence on uncertain resource markets.

5   John Kouwenhoven quoted in Jakle, *The Tourist*, 264.

Argyle Street, Port Alberni

Courtenay

Kamloops

Penticton

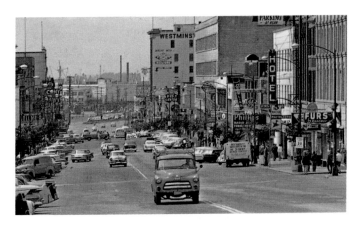

Columbia Street, New Westminster

Courtenay

Cache Creek

Kitimat

Burns Lake

Birch Avenue, 100 Mile House

Third Avenue, Prince George

Mile Zero Hotel, Dawson Creek

Williams Lake

George Street, Prince George

Granville Street Bridge

Vancouver Public Library

Vancouver International Airport

Granville Street and B.C. Electric Building

Simon Fraser University, North Burnaby

Queen Elizabeth Theatre

Bloedel Conservatory, Queen Elizabeth Park

Vancouver General Post Office

Granville Street

Granville Street

Fraser Arms Hotel

Fraser Arms Hotel

Marine Building

City Hall

Georgia Street Looking West

The Hudson's Bay Company Store

Entrance to Exhibition Park

Stanley Park Entrance to Lions Gate Bridge

Sports Tea Room, Stanley Park

Empress of Japan figurehead, Stanley Park

Brockton Point, Stanley Park

West End Apartments and Harbour

English Bay Beach

Sylvia Hotel at English Bay

Hotel Barclay, Port Alberni

Kelowna City Hall

Prince George Regional Hospital

Ingraham Hotel, Victoria

Provincial Government Building, Duncan

Foyer Maillard, Maillardville

Log Pond and Sawmill, Quesnel

INDUSTRY AND THE ENVIRONMENT

A POSTCARD OF THE LOG POND AND SAWMILL AT QUESNEL IS AN EXAMPLE of what might be thought of as the industrial sublime. Its billowing plume of black smoke, stacked pile of cut logs and crude, almost raw technology were intended to be read not just in terms of pride but also beauty. Celebrated as an essential part of the economic development that made good on the postwar era's promise of prosperity, the Quesnel sawmill is one of countless industrial sites and installations that were the subject of postcards during this period. From a contemporary perspective we might ask how an image that is this startling, even menacing, could have been read so uncritically. Ideological commitment to progress and simple pragmatism are part of it, but we might also refer back to the rise of the aesthetic appreciation of nature and its relationship to land as an economic resource. While there has never been a time in the history of modernity when nature and culture have not been deeply entangled, there has always been an urge, one could argue a need, to keep them separate or distinct. For all the images of heavy industry one finds during this period, they are countered and seemingly balanced by an instrumental vision of the province as a garden. A product of climate and geography as well as culture, the cultivation of nature in this form encompasses a wide variety of natural sites, wilderness and city parks as well as formal gardens, the latter reaching a kind of crescendo in the ornate floral arrangements and designs of the Butchart Gardens near Victoria.

Most industrial postcards emphasize the isolation of their subjects. As resource industries, these operations admittedly tend to be located in remote places or are situated to spearhead further development. Still, even where they exist in proximity to settlement or other forms of human activity, this is rarely depicted. Incorporating the unresolved tensions industrialization creates, the representation of these sites is generally placed safely at the margins of our everyday lives. A more complicated situation is represented by the town of Trail, where many of the contradictions that haunt the postcards in this book are forced into the open. Located in a mountainous pocket of the Kootenays in the southeastern interior of the province, Trail is probably best known for the Smoke Eaters, its senior men's hockey team that won a world amateur championship for Canada in the 1950s. The true glory of the place, however, is the smelter that inspired the team's proud but now ironic name. The fortunes of this company town have been tied to smelting since before the turn of the century. In 1951, with the postwar economy starting to heat up, Consolidated Mining and Smelting began a major expansion of its operations in Trail.

Over the next twenty years Trail's population peaked and the trappings of the good life were put in place.[1] The incredible physical and economic symbiosis of the smelting operations and the town, however, precluded the kind of separation that has been noted elsewhere. On the contrary, the identity of Trail and the smelter, whose sheer size and scale so dominates the town, merged in an image that boldly touted the benefits and opportunities associated with industrial development.

The tensions of trying to maintain this image are clearly apparent in a postcard from the 1960s.[2] In it, the smelter is pictured as a monumental presence in the distance from the vantage point provided by a colourful screen of flowers in a municipal park. By this time there was already sufficient environmental awareness that questions about the relationship of pollution and the quality of life were beginning to be raised. While measures have since been taken to ameliorate the effects of pollution in and around Trail, for many decades the landscape had been virtually barren of natural vegetation. The game is given away by the postcard's message: "Industry and environment . . . the beautiful Gardens of Gyro Park thrive in complete harmony with the world's largest lead and zinc smelting operations in Trail." A case of going on the attack when on the defensive, this card is a dramatic instance of the ideological rationalizations upon which the utopian images of modernity have been built. It is also a poignant reminder of how tenuous they are and why they can no longer be sustained.

It is with a somewhat earlier card, however, that the story of Trail might best conclude. Its set-up is not unlike the panoramic image of Rogers Pass discussed previously, but this card is rather less subtle. Overlooking both the great smelter and the desiccated landscape it produced, the stiffly posed viewers in this card are citizens of an age that hardly realizes it is almost already history. One can't help but make allusions to the classical temples that the towering smokestacks seem to evoke, or to recall that it is as ruins that we are fated to know them.

---

1   From 1951 to 1971 Trail maintained a population of more than 11,000 people. By 1981, however, it had dropped below 10,000 and, according to the 1991 census, stood at 7,919. See Barman, *The West Beyond the West*, p. 391.

2   It is not always possible to date postcards with entire accuracy. However, styles come and go in postcards like everything else. In the case of this card, it is in a slightly larger than usual format and its message appears in a white strip across the bottom of the image side of the card. This style mimics the look of John Hinde cards, which were widely imitated by the mid-1960s. (Please note: the portion of the card where the message appears is not reproduced in this publication.)

Pulpmill, Celgar Limited, Castlegar.

Log Booming Grounds, Vancouver Island

Pulpmill, Celgar Limited, Watson Island

The First Tower, Peace River Dam

Stanley Park, Vancouver

Sunken Gardens, The Butchart Gardens, Victoria

Delphiniums, The Butchart Gardens, Victoria

Industry and Environment

Cedar Avenue

Cominco Ammonia Plant and Sphere, Warfield

Commerce, Industry and Recreation unlimited

ILLUSTRATIONS

Entries include, in order: subject; publisher (and/or distributor), publisher's number; photographer; printer, printer's number. Not all of this information is indicated on all cards.

Many of these cards were produced by Grant-Mann Lithographers Ltd. of Vancouver. Grant-Mann was preceded by Mann Litho Co. Ltd. It was succeeded by Lawson-Jones Ltd., which also incorporated Smith Lithographers, followed by Lawson Graphics Pacific Ltd. and, currently, Lawson Mardon Packaging. The company both printed and published its own line of cards and produced and printed cards for other publishers, often under the "Traveltime" imprint. Abbreviations: GM — Grant-Mann; Mann — Mann Litho; Smith — Smith Lithographers; LG — Lawson Graphics.

Other abbreviations: LPS — Lakeside Photo Studios Ltd., Williams Lake; Taylor — G. Morris Taylor, Vancouver; NC — Natural Color Productions, Vancouver; Wilson — Alex Wilson Publications Ltd., Dryden, Ontario; Dexter — Dexter Color Canada Ltd., Cornwall, Ontario; Donaldson — R.L. Donaldson's Ltd., Cranbrook; D-WN — Dexter Press Inc., West Nyack, N.Y.; MA — Monahan Agency, Vernon; Process — New Process Colorcard, Victoria; VMS — Vancouver Magazine Service Ltd.; Wright — Stan V. Wright Ltd., Victoria; Hammitt — The Hammitt Company Ltd., Kelowna.